Glimpses of Church Life

An Exposition of Philemon

Malcolm Webber

Published by:

Strategic Press
Division of Strategic Global Assistance, Inc.
513 S. Main St. Suite 2
Elkhart, IN 46516
U.S.A.

Toll free: 1-844-532-3371 (1-844-LEADER1)

www.sgai.org

Our secure online bookstore: www.StrategicPress.org

ISBN: 978-1-888810-81-3

All Scripture references are from the English Standard Version of the Bible, unless otherwise noted.

Printed in the United States of America

Contents

Introduction

Philemon is not merely an example of how to skillfully make a difficult request of someone – although Paul demonstrates his mastery of that. But more than that, this is a wonderful letter about church life.

In Philemon we see many clear descriptions of what happened in the earliest churches and what their culture was like. While short, Philemon is a beautiful and deep articulation of healthy church life.

Philemon also gives a crystal clear picture of God's position on slavery; we have dedicated a chapter to this at the end.

To those who are pursuing a path back to true New Testament church life, we commit this brief exposition.

Malcolm Webber, Ph.D.
July 2020

Characters and Events in Philemon

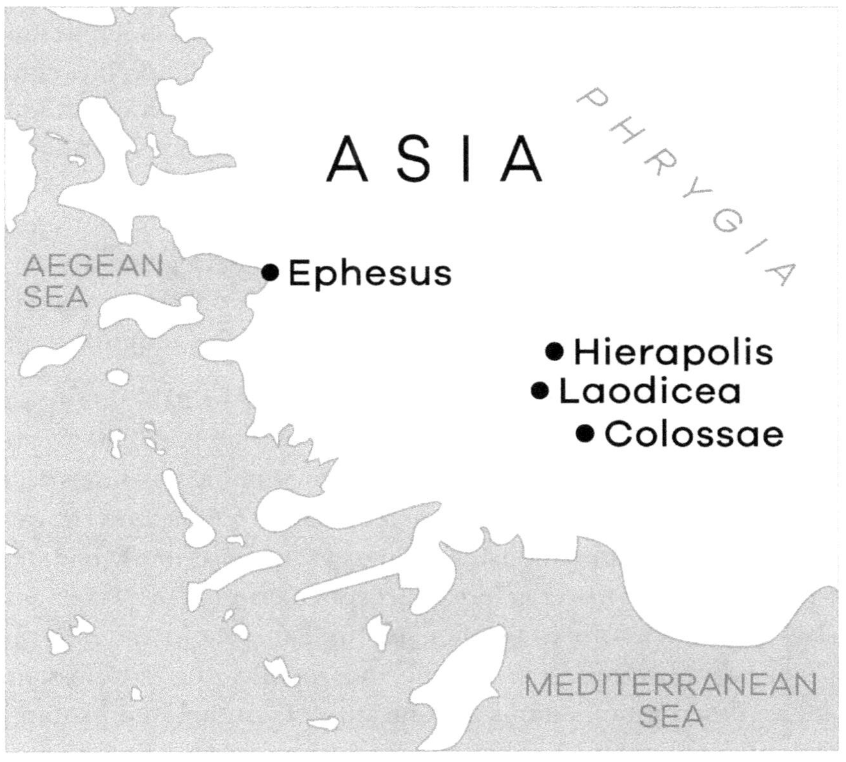

Philemon is the shortest and most personal of Paul's letters. The letter gives us a window into the life of a house church, as well as a beautiful picture of a wise handling of delicate relationships.

This letter is closely connected to Paul's letter to the Colossians. Onesimus was the carrier of both letters (along with Tychicus; Col. 4:7-9). Paul was a prisoner when he wrote this letter (vv. 1, 9-10, 23), possibly in Rome during his first imprisonment there.

The traditional assumption is that Philemon was a member of the Colossian church, which was part of the network of house churches in the three neighboring cities of Colossae, Laodicea and Hierapolis.

Philemon had originally come to Christ through Paul (v. 19). His slave Onesimus had possibly robbed him (v. 18) and fled to the city where Paul was – clearly without Philemon's approval. Onesimus thus became a runaway slave, and therefore was in great peril. If caught, runaway slaves were subject to severe beatings or even execution. In Roman times, the slave master's power was unlimited. He could mutilate, torture or kill the slave at his pleasure. Roman legislation imposed death for killing a plow-ox, but the murderer of a slave was not called to account. Tracking fugitive slaves was a legitimate trade. Recovered slaves might be branded on the forehead, condemned to hard labor, and even thrown to wild animals in the amphitheater.[1]

Onesimus eventually met and was led to Christ by Paul (v. 10); we don't know how they became connected. Onesimus then served Paul who nurtured his life in Christ. Paul was now sending Onesimus back to Colossae, and wanted him to be reconciled to Philemon but in a radically different relationship than what they previously had. He writes to Philemon asking him to accept Onesimus "no longer as a slave but … as a beloved brother" (v. 16). Paul sent his letter to the Colossian church at the same time and, significantly, in Colossians 4:9 he describes Onesimus as "our faithful and beloved brother" with no mention at all of his status as a former slave.

1 It was not until AD 312 that Rome passed a law declaring the killing of slaves by poisoning, throwing to wild animals, or other methods as homicide.

Because he is a runaway slave, Onesimus' return to Philemon is potentially dangerous for him. But with Paul as his spiritual father and advocate, Onesimus hopes for a good outcome. Moreover, Philemon has a good reputation for generosity in the community at Colossae so we can assume that Paul's request was met with a positive response.

In this letter, Paul demonstrates the profound change that the Gospel will make in a person's life. He also shows us that people who have received God's grace are to give that same grace to one another.

Specifically he asks Philemon to accept a new kind of relationship with Onesimus – one in which they are no longer master and slave, but brothers in the Lord (vv. 15-16). To do this will be a big step of generosity on Philemon's part as he is being asked to give up his worldly "property rights" to live appropriately in God's new family, the Church.

The fruit of all this may have been quite spectacular. Years later, Ignatius of Antioch wrote about a prominent leader called Onesimus in his Epistle to the Ephesians in AD 110. He called Onesimus "a man of inexpressible love" and said Onesimus "is your bishop, whom I pray you by Jesus Christ to love, and that you would all seek to be like him. Blessed be God, who has granted unto you, who are yourselves so excellent, to obtain such an excellent bishop."[2]

While Onesimus was a fairly common name for a slave, it is unlikely that many slaves would have risen to such a prominent leadership role in the church at Ephesus. We cannot know for sure, but it is possible that this is the same Onesimus Paul writes about in his letter to Philemon. If Onesimus were a young man at the time he met

2 Ignatius of Antioch. (1885). The Epistle of Ignatius to the Ephesians. In A. Roberts, J. Donaldson, & A. C. Coxe (Eds.), *The Apostolic Fathers with Justin Martyr and Irenaeus* (Vol. 1, p. 49). Buffalo, NY: Christian Literature Company.

Paul, he would have been in his seventies when he knew Ignatius in AD 110.[3]

If this were true, it would help explain the preservation of Paul's letter to Philemon and its inclusion in the New Testament canon.[4] It would also provide a tremendous testimony to the power of Paul's leader development work in building a young runaway slave (the lowest of the low in a highly stratified society) into a mighty leader in the church. It attests not only to Paul's work but also to that of Philemon, and the church in his home, who would have continued to invest in Onesimus upon his return to them.

The message of Philemon is needed by the whole family of God, both then and now and in all cultures of the world. It is a profound, practical teaching that would become the precedent for all believers everywhere in all of the Roman world, and would then have continuing application for the Christian family until the present day.

The truth of "neither slave nor free in Christ" had to begin at some point in the life of the Church, and it is in the context of receiving Onesimus that this now became established as the settled norm for all followers of the Lord Jesus (1 Cor. 12:13; Gal. 3:28; Eph. 6:8; Col. 3:11).

---

3 According to church tradition, Onesimus was later martyred in Rome during the time of Trajan the emperor.

4 It is likely that Paul wrote many personal letters to people. He was a writer and he had many friends and a lot to say! But most of his letters were not preserved or included in the New Testament.

The Book of Philemon

1-3 THE GREETING

1 Paul, a prisoner for Christ Jesus, and Timothy our brother, To Philemon our beloved fellow worker

a prisoner for Christ Jesus

Refers to Paul's literal imprisonment (vv. 9, 23), but also to his complete dedication to Christ.

Paul does not describe himself as "Paul, the apostle" as he does in the companion letter to the Colossians (Col. 1:1) and elsewhere. Here he is not speaking authoritatively, but as a friend. He is about to ask a big favor of Philemon; in preparation for that he assumes a low position. In addition, he is subtly identifying with the slave whom he wants Philemon to embrace as a forgiven brother and co-worker.

This is the only time in Paul's letters that he refers to himself in the greeting as a "prisoner for Christ." Nevertheless, being a prisoner of Christ is still obviously an honorable designation in the church!

To Philemon

The letter is primarily addressed to Philemon.[5]

Philemon our beloved fellow worker

Paul had never been to Colossae (Col. 2:1) so it is possible he had never met Philemon but still loved him as a fellow worker in Christ. Alternatively, Philemon may have met Paul when Paul was in Ephesus – Colossae is about 100 miles east of Ephesus – and may have been led to Christ by Paul there.

Moreover, Paul was deeply connected to Philemon through Epaphras, Paul's spiritual son, who had planted the church in Colossae (Col. 1:7).

2 and Apphia our sister and Archippus our fellow soldier, and the church in your house:

Apphia

Perhaps she was Philemon's wife, or possibly a leader in the church, or both.

Archippus our fellow soldier

A leader in the church. In Colossians 4:17, Paul exhorts Archippus to "fulfill the ministry that you have received in the Lord."

Apphia ... and Archippus ... and the church

This is a personal letter but it is not private. The letter is to and about Philemon, but Paul also addresses Apphia, Archippus and

5 The singular "you" in verses 4, 6-8, 10-12, 16, 18-21 and 23 obviously refers to Philemon. "You" and "your" is plural only in verses 3, 22 and 25.

the church that meets in Philemon's house (v. 2). In this way, Paul turns a private matter into a matter of concern to the whole local church family, who thus become a witness both to Paul's request and also to Philemon's response.

Onesimus is now a part of the family of God, and not only Philemon's household. Therefore, Paul makes Philemon accountable to the whole church family in this matter. In addition, Paul wants the church to know about Onesimus' good standing with him and he wants the entire church to embrace him as a brother and no longer as a slave. This is a picture of family life in the Church.

the church in your house

The Early Church had no "church buildings" at all and met usually in private homes (Acts 12:12; 1 Cor. 16:19; Rom. 16:5; Col. 4:15).[6]

your house

Philemon is a man of some means since his house is big enough to host a local gathering of believers. He was probably a patron of the church, like Phoebe (Rom. 16:1-2). He was also a practical blessing to many saints (v. 7).

---

6 The Dura-Europos church in Syria is the earliest identified Christian house church. It was apparently a normal domestic house converted for religious services (it had a baptistry, altar and religious art) sometime between 233 and 256. (Provance, B. S. (2009). In *Pocket Dictionary of Liturgy & Worship* (p. 51). Downers Grove, IL: IVP Academic.) The Aqaba Church in Jordan is considered to be the world's oldest purpose-built Christian church, dated between 293 and 303. (Govier, G. (1998). Archaeology: "Oldest Church" Discovered in Jordan. *Christianity Today, 42*(10), 26.)

3 Grace to you and peace from God our Father and the Lord Jesus Christ.

Grace to you and peace

Paul's common greeting in many of his letters. However, this was not merely a routine greeting; it had profound meaning for Paul. We are transformed into a true family by the extension of grace and peace to us from God!

4-7 AFFIRMATION AND PRAYER FOR PHILEMON

4 I thank my God always when I remember you in my prayers,

I thank my God always

For Paul, prayer and thanksgiving were closely connected (Rom. 1:8; 1 Cor. 1:4; Eph. 1:16; Phil. 1:3; Col. 1:3; 1 Thess. 1:2; 2 Thess. 1:3).

Every letter of Paul's, except his urgent letter to the Galatians, begins with thanksgiving.

5 because I hear of your love and of the faith that you have toward the Lord Jesus and for all the saints,

I thank my God … because I hear of your love and … faith

The grace of God was the source of Philemon's love and faith so Paul thanked God for the fruit in Philemon's life.

I hear

Paul would have heard about Philemon from Epaphras (v. 23; Col. 1:8) and possibly even Onesimus.

I hear of your love and ... faith

Before getting to his request, Paul begins with a beautiful affirmation of Philemon – specifically of his faith toward God and his love toward the saints (as in Col. 1:4).

for all the saints

In the Body of Christ, all are equally loved by God and all must be equally loved by each other – whether Jew or Gentile, and here, very importantly, slave or free.

6 and I pray that the sharing of your faith may become effective for the full knowledge of every good thing that is in us for the sake of Christ.

This is the hardest verse in the letter to translate and it has been translated in a variety of ways, none of which is bad.

I pray that

Paul now gives us the content of his prayer.

sharing

The Greek word is κοινωνία (*koinonia*) and means, broadly, "fellowship," "relationship," "partnership." Here it probably has the sense of "participation" – "that your participation in the faith may become effective ..."[7]

By *koinonia,* Paul has a very big thing in view. First, he means our participation in Christ – knowing God, loving God, experiencing

7 Arndt, W., Danker, F. W., Bauer, W., & Gingrich, F. W. (2000). *A Greek-English Lexicon of the New Testament and Other Early Christian Literature* (3rd ed., p. 553). Chicago: University of Chicago Press.

God – union with Christ and all that includes. Second, he means our participation in knowing God with one another – our union *together* with Christ and all that includes.

> Christian unity is not a unity of structure, but of fellowship. It is not merely an outward identification with other Christians or churches or movements. It is a living, spiritual union.
>
> When we speak of "fellowship" in this context, we do not mean superficial relationships, but Divine fellowship. We are not referring to mere friendliness or co-operation, or just doing things together. We mean a living, spiritual fellowship; participating in the life of Jesus in each other; beholding Him in one another; touching Him, and being touched by Him, through each other. It is a fellowship that proceeds spontaneously from the overflowing reality of the indwelling Presence of Jesus Christ in our hearts and lives.
>
> It is through true spiritual fellowship with each other that we are touched by Him; and when His hand touches us, we are changed. This is how the saints minister to each other for the building up of the Body of Christ. This is how "the whole body [is] joined and held together by every joint with which it is equipped." This is the operation of the Church "when each part is working properly." This is what "makes the body grow so that it builds itself up in love" (Eph. 4:12-16).
>
> This is the process of corporate spiritual maturity. This is Christ dwelling in the hearts of His people, in ever-increasing revelation of Himself. This is all the saints coming to the experiential knowledge of the fullness of His love. This is the Church which will soon be "filled with all the fullness of God" (Eph. 3:17-19). And it is through fellowship.

Again, by "fellowship" we do not mean shallow friendships, but intimate, spiritual friendships; spiritual communion; the expression of Divine life within God's people.

Christian fellowship is a heart to heart, "deep calls to deep," intimate spiritual communion. It is a profound perception of Jesus Christ in one another; enjoying Jesus in each other. It is a receiving from Him through each other; a giving of Him one to another. It is fellowshipping with Him – together. It is participation in the eternal fellowship of the Godhead – together. It is participation in the everlasting love of the Godhead – together.

Think of the eternal fellowship of the Father, Son and Holy Spirit. Think of the joyful, loving, living, abundant fellowship within the Godhead. That is the life of His Church.

Jesus gave us a new commandment:

> *… that you love one another: just as I have loved you, you also are to love one another. (John 13:34)*

Our love for each other is to be "just as" Jesus loved us. How could we love one another with Jesus' love, unless He Himself were abiding within us to love? And how could our brother be worthy of such love, except Jesus were abiding in him to receive it?

> *… as you did it to one of the least of these My brothers, you did it to Me. (Matt. 25:40)*

As we love one another, we love Him. As we enjoy one another, we enjoy Him. In caring for each other, we care for Him. In opening our hearts and lives to one another, we invite His Presence. In serving each other, we kiss His feet. In pouring out our lives for one another, we pour out His love back to Him. As we prefer one another, we give Him the pre-eminence. As we behold each other, we perceive His beauty. As we embrace one another with self-giving love, we taste His sweetness. As we wash each other's feet, we smell His fragrance.

Jesus dwells in His Church – to love and to be loved. As we love one another, quickly and imperceptibly the one love passes over into the other, and we love Him. As we fellowship with each other, quietly and almost unnoticeably we come in contact with Him. And the loving fellowship with which we embrace our brother ascends to that with which we love God, and we are united together in the eternal love and fellowship of the Godhead.

> *... if we love one another, God abides in us and His love is perfected in us. (1 John 4:12)*

Church life is both a foretaste and a beginning of everlasting life. As we love one another, we participate in the eternal love and fellowship of the Godhead, joyfully awaiting the fullness of this union, in the realm which is to come.[8]

effective for the full knowledge of every good thing

That you will know and experience every blessing that we receive in Christ – that you will come into His fullness!

that is in us

Through our union with Christ we have every good thing "in us" (Eph. 1:3; 2 Pet. 1:3). "Us" includes the whole church at Colossae; it includes all who have received God's grace, including Onesimus.

---

8 From *In Him Was Life* by Malcolm Webber (1991).

for the sake of Christ

The preposition εἰς (eis) means, "into," "in," "toward." Its use here could mean "for the glory of Christ," or "into the fullness of union with Christ" – certainly both meanings are true of who we are in Christ. Paul's primary meaning is probably in line with his words to the Ephesians: "until we all attain to the unity of the faith and of the knowledge of the Son of God, to mature manhood, to the measure of the stature of the fullness of Christ" (Eph. 4:13).

Essentially, Paul hears how well Philemon is doing (v. 5) and then prays in verse 6 that he will continue to grow into the completeness of everything God has for him. This includes the fullness of the Christian life – Philemon's union with Christ, faith, love and generosity toward others (particularly toward Onesimus).

7 For I have derived much joy and comfort from your love, my brother, because the hearts of the saints have been refreshed through you.

For

A further reason for Paul's thanksgiving in verse 4, and a further ground for his prayer of verse 6.

I have derived much joy and comfort from your love

Philemon's love and generosity toward the saints have given Paul much joy and comfort. As a spiritual father, Paul's heart is filled when he hears that his children are doing well. In fact, there is no greater joy (3 John 4)!

my brother

Paul speaks affectionately in a familial way, as he so often does to the people of God.

refreshed

The saints have been blessed through Philemon's encouragement, hospitality and various practical blessings. Not only were their needs supplied, but their hearts were also refreshed by him.

refreshed through you

Philemon has a reputation for generosity. Now, in front of the church, that reputation will be tested by Paul's request for Onesimus' freedom.

The risk of Philemon declining Paul's request is probably small. He has proven himself as a gracious and hospitable man. With Paul's specific encouragement here, no doubt he will do well regarding Onesimus.

This is an affirmation of the central place of generosity in the life of the church. We are to be generous in everything – in kindness, in encouragement, in money, in hospitality, and now in giving freedom to a slave!

Philemon is already a generous man; there is no question about that. So, Paul's appeal is not so much to prompt him to be generous, but rather to persuade him to overturn the long-established social custom of slavery. The Church is called to be different from the world and this takes courage!

8-12 PAUL'S APPEAL FOR ONESIMUS

Paul now comes to his purpose for writing this letter: to restore Onesimus to Philemon and to gain Philemon's forgiveness for his runaway slave.

8 Accordingly, though I am bold enough in Christ to command you to do what is required,

Accordingly

In other words: Since you are a very generous person who refreshes the hearts of God's people (v. 7), therefore I appeal to you to be generous in this also (vv. 8f). Philemon has shown exemplary love to God's people and that love should now extend to his runaway slave.

I am bold enough in Christ

Paul was so clear about what he believed that he had no hesitation in being blunt and open. He knew he was right in asking for Onesimus to be set free. Moreover, he had the authority in Christ to make this demand.

On one hand, he was declining to command Philemon to free Onesimus; on the other hand, saying that he declined to command him was itself a clear expression of his expectation.

command

Paul could have required this of Philemon on the basis of Paul's leading him to Christ and eternal life. He prefers, instead, to entreat him as a friend and co-worker.

Thus, Paul sets aside his own personal rights by way of example to Philemon, who he is asking to do the same. Just as Paul doesn't use his own power to compel Philemon but instead allows Philemon the freedom to make his own decision, so he asks Philemon to do the same, declining to exercise his power over Onesimus but instead allowing Onesimus to be free to follow God's call on his life.

In the Church we are to lay down our own rights, preferring our brothers and sisters as "more significant" than ourselves (Phil. 2:1-11). In doing this, we will empower one another to serve God freely.

what is required

The Greek word means what is proper or fitting. It was the right thing for Philemon to set Onesimus free and receive him as a brother, equal in Christ (Gal. 3:28).

9 yet for love's sake I prefer to appeal to you – I, Paul, an old man and now a prisoner also for Christ Jesus –

yet

Instead of commanding you, I will appeal to you.

for love's sake

For the sake of Paul's love to Philemon and what should be Philemon's love to Onesimus, his brother in Christ.

I prefer to appeal to you

Paul desires that Philemon will do this on his own initiative (with some prompting) rather than out of compulsion.

True reconciliation will occur only when conflicted parties each take the initiative to resolve it, rather than out of duress.

an old man and now a prisoner also for Christ Jesus

Socially and economically, Paul was not Philemon's equal, but as his spiritual father in the faith – especially as "an old man" and "a prisoner also for Christ Jesus" – he appeals to him.

Paul intentionally describes his own weakness and vulnerability. In making his request, he puts himself "lower" than the one he's appealing to. He identifies with the powerless. At the same time, both his age and his service to Christ give Paul considerable stature.

In addition, Paul elicits some sympathy for himself as a prisoner, and, indirectly, for Onesimus who is also a prisoner of slavery.

old man

Paul was probably about 60, although it is impossible to know his age exactly.[9] With all of his labor and hardship Paul would have been an "old 60."

---

9 Paul was a "young man" about 30 years previously at the stoning of Stephen (Acts 7:58); perhaps around 30 or less at that time. According to the sixth-century BC Greek physician Hippocrates, the Greek word used here for "old man" applied to an individual between 49 and 56.

10 I appeal to you for my child, Onesimus, whose father I became in my imprisonment.

appeal

Implore or entreat. "Please do this."

my child, Onesimus

Onesimus became a believer through Paul, just as Philemon had. He was originally from Colossae (Col. 4:9).

"Onesimus" literally means "useful," "profitable" or "beneficial." It was a common name for slaves at that time, chosen by the slave owners for them, pragmatically and demeaningly[10] – although not confined to them.

This is the first and only time Onesimus is named in the letter. He is also named in Colossians 4:7-9 as being one of the party from Paul who came with that letter for the church.

It is significant that Paul waits so long to name Onesimus, who is the main point of the letter; in fact, the name Onesimus is the last word in the verse in the Greek! J. B. Phillips paraphrases Paul's words as: "Yes, I have become a father though I have been under lock and key, and the child's name is – Onesimus!" First, Paul wisely wanted to gain favor with Philemon.

Paul is so careful in this letter. Since Onesimus was the one carrying the letter to Philemon, Philemon had no chance to think about this in advance. In addition, this letter may have been read in front of the church (v. 2) – including the other slaves in Philemon's household! Facing Onesimus, Philemon would need to decide his response immediately.

---

10 According to Aristotle, a slave was an "instrument of action" or "a tool with life in it."

whose father I became

The Greek is literally, "who I fathered." Paul "begat" Onesimus.[11]

Christian leaders are spiritual fathers and mothers (1 Cor. 4:14-15; Gal. 4:9; 1 Tim. 1:2; 2 Tim. 1:2; Tit. 1:4). They are not corporate executives. Paul is very affectionate toward Onesimus.

Leaders build leaders! Every true leader, no matter how important they become, must always be personally reaching out to the next generation, building their lives.

This is a strong request: "Onesimus is my child; I am his father. I appeal to you for my child!"

imprisonment

Literally, "bonds" as in chains or ropes (see Eph. 6:20). Presumably, Paul led Onesimus to Christ when he was in prison. We do not know the circumstances.

11 (Formerly he was useless to you, but now he is indeed useful to you and to me.)

useless ... useful

A play on words with Onesimus' name "useful." The word came from the verb "to profit" or "to benefit," which appears in verse 20, another play on words.[12]

---

11 Ironically, in his old age (v. 9)!

12 Such plays upon proper names were common both in Greek and Roman literature.

he was useless to you

Perhaps refers to Onesimus stealing from Philemon and then running away.[13] "Useless" is a mild euphemism, since verse 18 implies that Onesimus had actually "wronged" Philemon.

useful to you and to me

It's not clear what Paul's ultimate hope was – whether he wanted Onesimus to stay with Philemon in a new relationship of brotherly equality, or whether he hoped Philemon would send Onesimus back to help him. Either way, Paul is benefited – with the joy of Philemon's setting Onesimus free or with the benefit of receiving Onesimus back to himself.

If the church tradition is true, and this was the Onesimus who eventually became the top leader of the church at Ephesus, then he was useful indeed!

In some ways there is a parallel between John Mark in relation to Paul and Onesimus in relation to Philemon. After their initial separation (Acts 15:37-40), John Mark has now been restored to Paul (Col. 4:10). Perhaps Paul had applied what he is now teaching Philemon to his own treatment of Mark, for he eventually described John Mark as "very useful" to him – the Greek word for "useful" in 2 Timothy 4:11 is identical to the word used here. This is an important leadership lesson. Many times, the one who was formerly not suitable now becomes invaluable. Someone whom we had once dismissed as unprofitable can be brought back to ministry to be powerfully used by God.

---

13 Many slave owners stereotyped slaves as lazy and ill-disciplined – especially Phrygian slaves, as Onesimus was.

12 I am sending him back to you, sending my very heart.

sending my very heart

Paul loves Onesimus as his own son. Moreover, Paul is being gently persuasive. He is sending back a very part of himself!

13-16 ONESIMUS' NEW LIFE IN CHRIST

13 I would have been glad to keep him with me, in order that he might serve me on your behalf during my imprisonment for the Gospel,

glad to keep him with me

This is a great affirmation of Onesimus. Paul entirely trusts him and wants him to stay and help.

with me

The Greek preposition is πρός (*pros*) and means more than simply near or beside. It implies fellowship.

serve me on your behalf

Paul speaks almost as if Philemon had sent Onesimus to help him! This also implies that Philemon is obligated to Onesimus, since Onesimus served Paul in his place. Onesimus did what Philemon did not do.

during my imprisonment

This is the fourth time Paul mentions his imprisonment.

Paul would have needed practical assistance in his imprisonment. Timothy was also with Paul (v. 1), but Paul was regularly sending him away on assignments. Epaphroditus had been sent by the Philippian church to help Paul in a similar way (Phil. 2:25). Thus, Onesimus was not a slave to Paul performing only menial duties; he was a spiritual son and a helper, no doubt also including ministry work.

14 but I preferred to do nothing without your consent in order that your goodness might not be by compulsion but of your own accord.

but I preferred

Paul wanted to keep Onesimus but chose to send him back.

your consent

Onesimus' future is in Philemon's hands.

in order that your goodness

This clearly implies that Philemon will do the right thing and release Onesimus.

your goodness

It is not clear whether Paul wants Philemon to send Onesimus back to help him or to forgive Onesimus and have him remain in his own household as an equal brother in Christ. In either case, it would be a "good" thing.

compulsion

Paul doesn't want Philemon to respond out of pressure, but from his heart. True generosity is always from a willing heart and never forced (2 Cor. 9:5, 7).

accord

The Greek word means voluntarily, of his own free will.

Paul could have simply kept Onesimus and informed Philemon about it. Instead, he gave Philemon this opportunity to do the right thing and release his slave. This was a challenging assignment for Philemon – one that he no doubt accomplished.

15 For this perhaps is why he was parted from you for a while, that you might have him back forever,

For

This is another reason why Paul decided not to keep Onesimus with him: it is God who has allowed all of this to save Onesimus and then for him to return to Philemon as a brother.

perhaps

Paul certainly believes in God's providence in the whole thing. But he speaks softly here to again relieve the sense of pressure.

he was parted from you

The verb uses the passive voice: he was parted or separated. This is a very gentle way of describing the fact that Onesimus ran away! Ultimately, it was God's act, brought about, or at least overruled, by Him.

that you might have him back forever

Paul was such a visionary! He sees God's highest purpose in this situation and appeals to Philemon to do the same.

Onesimus left his former circumstances as a slave possessed by Philemon, but he returned to Philemon now as a believer possessed by God!

a while … forever

This is a beautiful contrast. They have only temporarily been separated but, in Christ, will be together for eternity. Paul now speaks of their new relationship as Christian brothers.

forever

The Greek word is αἰώνιος (*aionios*), the normal word in the New Testament that refers to eternity.

16 no longer as a bondservant but more than a bondservant, as a beloved brother – especially to me, but how much more to you, both in the flesh and in the Lord.

no longer as a bondservant

God deals with slavery here very clearly – in the Church, it is to be "no longer"!

Paul's letter to Philemon shows us that social hierarchies, such as the one between a master and his powerless slave, are dismantled in Christ (see also Eph. 2:11-22).

a bondservant

The Greek word (δοῦλος, *doulos*) in this historical and socio-economic context is much better translated as "slave."[14]

14 The Greek word δοῦλος (*doulos*) is often translated as "servant" or "bondservant" in the New Testament but here should certainly be "slave."

Fundamentally, Paul's letter to Philemon is a beautiful revelation of God's heart toward the slave. Please see the later section on "God and Slavery" for a detailed analysis of slavery in Paul's day and the Early Church's response.

as a beloved brother

Onesimus left as a slave but returns as a beloved brother.

Paul abolishes any "sacred-secular" divide here. Such a divide would make it possible for Philemon and Onesimus to be brethren on Sunday but master and slave for the rest of the week. Paul does not allow that artificial divide. If we are brothers in Christ, then we are brothers all week long!

Just as the Christian life is all our life, so church life does not only happen during a Sunday meeting but it is all week long.

This is also why it is appropriate for Paul to make his appeal to Philemon in front of the church (v. 2). This is not only a private matter between Philemon and Onesimus, but a corporate matter for the whole church to know and affirm.

Finally, it should be noted that for Philemon to set Onesimus free simply on the basis of his Christian faith and the recognition that he and Onesimus were one in Christ, would have been an extraordinary and quite radical act in that day. This is not a small thing that Paul is asking. Indeed, the Christian life and church life are a profound departure from the norm in every way!

as a beloved brother … to me … to you

Paul puts all three men on the same level now – equal in Christ.

especially to me

Onesimus was a beloved brother to Paul because he was Paul's convert and because he had served Paul so well.

how much more to you

Onesimus should be loved by Philemon even more than he is by Paul because he is so much nearer to Philemon and in a longer-term relationship. Moreover, Philemon is like the father of the prodigal son who rejoices so greatly that his son has returned.

both in the flesh and in the Lord

Onesimus will be dear to Philemon both as a man ("in the flesh") who now has a new relationship to Philemon – no longer as a slave but as an equal – and as a brother in the Lord.

17-21 SECOND APPEAL

---

17 So if you consider me your partner, receive him as you would receive me.

So

Paul returns to his main point from verse 12 – his request for Philemon to forgive and release Onesimus. The next few verses are the climax of the whole letter.

if you consider me your partner

The Greek has the sense of, "I assume that you do" – "since you consider me your partner."

partner

The Greek word is from the same root as κοινωνία (*koinonia*) that is used in verse 6. Paul and Philemon are one in Christ and one in the same shared ministry, vision and purpose. This is a deep appeal to Philemon: "If we are one in Christ then receive Onesimus as you would receive me."

receive him as you would receive me

We know that Philemon would receive Paul with the utmost respect, care, love and blessing. He is now to do the same for Onesimus.

Conversely, for Philemon to reject Onesimus would be the same as rejecting Paul, which would be unthinkable.

Paul shows us here what leadership "power" looks like in the Kingdom. Paul never uses his power for his own benefit but always to bless and empower others (Matt. 20:28). Here he uses his power for the benefit of Onesimus.

With these words, Paul again breaks the back of slavery.

18 If he has wronged you at all, or owes you anything, charge that to my account.

If he has wronged you

The Greek has the sense of, "I assume that he has." It was common for a runaway slave to take some valuables or money from his master. Moreover, Onesimus would have told Paul what had happened.

Paul knows the situation – that Philemon was wronged by Onesimus – but he gives Philemon the opportunity to overlook that he was in fact wronged by Onesimus. Paul anticipates that Philemon will be generous in forgiving Onesimus just as he has been generous in so many other ways.

wronged you … owes you anything

We don't know what this refers to. Perhaps Onesimus stole from Philemon when he left. "Owes" is a very delicate way of referring to theft!

charge

An accounting term.

my account

Paul accepts the responsibility for any indebtedness of Onesimus to Philemon. This is symbolic. Paul's account with Philemon was limitless (v. 19); Philemon would never ask Paul to pay him back anything. In effect, Paul asks him to completely forgive Onesimus and to allow himself to have been wronged (1 Cor. 6:1-8).

19 I, Paul, write this with my own hand: I will repay it – to say nothing of your owing me even your own self.

I, Paul, write this with my own hand

In a sense, Paul is personally signing this promise, making himself "legally" obligated to it. It is a formal commitment, even though Paul knows that Philemon won't ask for anything.

with my own hand

It seems at this point, Paul took the stylus and signed his name (1 Cor. 16:21; Gal. 6:11; Col. 4:18; 2 Thess. 3:17), his chains running over the paper as he did so.

to say nothing of your owing me

A gentle reminder. This is like the English idiom, "not to mention that," in which the speaker does in fact mention what he says he will not mention.

your owing me even your own self

Paul contrasts the tiny debt Onesimus owes Philemon with the eternal debt that Philemon owes Paul. Jesus drew this same contrast in Matthew 18:21-35. In effect, Paul says, "I am now indebted to you; but don't forget that your debt to me is far greater – you owe me your very life."

There is a deep revelation of substitution, forgiveness and reconciliation here. Paul assumed Onesimus' debt just as Jesus assumed ours on the Cross (Is. 53:6). Then Paul does not even mention Onesimus' sin – just as God "forgets" ours (Heb. 8:12) and then requires us to forgive all those who have wronged us. This is the basis for the reconciliation in Christ now between Philemon and Onesimus.

We don't know for sure, but it's possible that Paul personally led Philemon to the Lord during his time in Ephesus. But it's also possible, although less likely, that Paul sees Philemon as the fruit of his ministry at Colossae through Paul's spiritual son Epaphras.

In his letter to the Colossians, the distant way in which Paul wrote that he had "heard" of their faith (Col. 1:4) and his description of them as never having seen him face to face (Col. 2:1) imply that he neither founded the church in Colossae nor had visited it. Quite likely, Epaphras founded the church (Col. 1:6-7). Epaphras was with Paul at the time of this writing (Col. 4:12-13). Possibly, Epaphras was a convert of Paul's ministry in Ephesus and had planted the church at Colossae. Appropriately, Paul assumed a certain authority over the Colossian church in his letter to them and now in his letter to Philemon, even though he had never been there, since he is a "grandfather" of the work through his spiritual son Epaphras.

20 Yes, brother, I want some benefit from you in the Lord. Refresh my heart in Christ.

Yes, brother

"Yes" adds emphasis to Paul's appeal. "Brother" reinforces the affectionate bond between Paul and Philemon. In effect Paul says, "I repeat, dear brother."

I want some benefit from you

When Philemon is generous toward Onesimus, Paul will take that as a personal benefit.

benefit

This is a play on words since the name Onesimus ("Useful") is from the same root as this verb.

Fifty years later, Ignatius of Antioch used the same play on words. In his letter to the church of Ephesus, Ignatius mentioned the bishop of Ephesus, who had the name Onesimus, and using the same verbal form and sentence construction as Paul uses here, said to the believers at Ephesus, "May I always have 'profit' of you, if indeed I be worthy of it."[15]

in the Lord

This will be appropriate since we are united together in Christ.

---

15 Ignatius of Antioch. (1885). The Epistle of Ignatius to the Ephesians, 2:2. In A. Roberts, J. Donaldson, & A. C. Coxe (Eds.), *The Apostolic Fathers with Justin Martyr and Irenaeus* (Vol. 1, p. 50). Buffalo, NY: Christian Literature Company.

Refresh my heart

Paul will have great joy and encouragement when Philemon responds well.

Refresh

This is the same word as in verse 7. "Just as you have refreshed the hearts of the saints with your generosity toward them, now refresh my heart with your generosity toward Onesimus."

21 Confident of your obedience, I write to you, knowing that you will do even more than I say.

Confident of your obedience

This would have been a hard request to refuse! In addition, Paul knew that Philemon was a mature man of God, gracious and generous. He's quite sure Philemon will respond well to his appeal.

your obedience

This is the strongest word so far that Paul uses for Philemon's anticipated response. The implication is that Philemon will be obedient to God in doing the right thing.

you will do even more than I say

Paul is not clear about what this might involve. Certainly he expects Philemon to set Onesimus free. Perhaps he also hopes that Philemon will send Onesimus back to help him (v. 13). Either way, he wants this initiative to come from Philemon, rather than telling him what to do.

22 REQUEST FOR HOSPITALITY

22 At the same time, prepare a guest room for me, for I am hoping that through your prayers I will be graciously given to you.

At the same time

In other words, "One more thing ..."

prepare a guest room for me

Paul asks for a simpler gift than Onesimus' freedom – he asks for hospitality when he is released from his current imprisonment.

It is not explicitly connected here, but the fact of Paul's coming visit would create an additional sense of accountability for Philemon. Paul will know how Onesimus was treated.

The "guest room" indicates Philemon's financial status.[16] However, it was not just a single room Paul was asking for. The Greek word could be translated "lodging" or "hospitality." There will be others traveling with Paul, so this is an implied request for them also.

16 It is likely that Philemon had a very large home. Four centuries later, Christians claimed to know its location. Theodoret, Bishop of Cyrrhus AD 423 – c. 466, says in the preface to his commentary on Philemon that Philemon's house had survived to his own day. (Bruce, F. F. (1984). *The Epistles to the Colossians, to Philemon, and to the Ephesians* (p. 222). Grand Rapids, MI: Wm. B. Eerdmans Publishing Co.)

through your prayers

This was not merely politeness. Paul really believed in the power of their prayers. Moreover, he needed God to move on his behalf so he would be set free. Many were praying for Paul; he constantly requested it (Rom. 15:30; 2 Cor. 1:11; Phil. 1:19; 1 Thess. 5:25; 2 Thess. 3:1).

I will be graciously given to you

Paul's coming visit is described as being a "gift" to Philemon and the church. Paul was deeply loved by them. Moreover, he was their spiritual father.

23-26 FINAL GREETINGS AND BLESSING

---

23 Epaphras, my fellow prisoner in Christ Jesus, sends greetings to you,

Epaphras

Epaphras gets the first and special mention because he is from Colossae and started the work in Colossae, Hierapolis, and Laodicea (Col. 1:7; 4:12). He came to Paul to enlist his help against the various errors that were attacking the church in Colossae, and Paul wrote his letter to the Colossians in response.

Mentioning Epaphras, and the others in verse 24, also gently adds to the pressure on Philemon. Not only will the church at Colossae know about all of this but Paul's companions do too!

my fellow prisoner

This means either that Epaphras was also imprisoned with Paul or simply, and perhaps more likely, that he was staying with Paul voluntarily, sharing his imprisonment as a companion. Aristarchus is also called "my fellow prisoner" in Colossians 4:10.

24 and so do Mark, Aristarchus, Demas, and Luke, my fellow workers.

Mark

This is probably John Mark (Acts 12:25; Col. 4:10; 2 Tim. 4:11), the writer of the Gospel. He is called a spiritual "son" of Peter's in 1 Peter 5:13.

Aristarchus

Aristarchus was a Thessalonian (Acts 19:29; 20:4; 27:2) and traveled with Paul for a while.

Aristarchus and Mark, along with "Jesus who is called Justus," were the only Jewish members of Paul's team (Col. 4:10-11).

Demas

Demas is mentioned in Colossians 4:14 and, very sadly, in 2 Timothy 4:10.

Luke

This is the beloved physician (Col. 4:14) and writer of the Gospel and Acts. Luke was faithful to Paul until the very end (2 Tim. 4:11).

my fellow workers

They are members of Paul's apostolic team. They are all named in detail in Colossians 4:10-14 with positive words about them. "Jesus who is called Justus" is additionally named there; we don't know why he's not named here.

Elsewhere, Paul named many more "fellow workers": Epaphroditus (Phil. 2:25), Euodia, Syntyche and Clement (Phil. 4:2-3), Titus (2 Cor.

8:23), Priscilla and Aquila (Rom. 16:3), Urbanus (Rom. 16:9), Silas (1 Thess. 1:1; 2:6), and, of course, Timothy (Rom. 16:21; 1 Tim 1:2).

In contrast to many Christian leaders today, Paul was not a "lone ranger" celebrity leader. He lived and served in community. He was deeply committed to his own spiritual community. He had led some of them to Christ, he built them all in the faith, he mentored them in their callings, and he sent them out with major assignments, all along supporting them and their work. Moreover, their love, fellowship and support sustained Paul as well. Like Jesus Himself (Mark 14:37), Paul needed his friends and fellow workers. He was a healthy leader.

Incidentally, all of these fellow workers – including Epaphras who began the work in Colossae – are also anticipating Onesimus' liberation! Without directly putting pressure on Philemon, Paul certainly knew how to do it indirectly. Philemon did not necessarily need to be pressured to do the right thing; his godliness and generosity were thoroughly proven. However, the institution of slavery was so deeply established in the culture and this was such a radical new kind of request, that Paul gave many gentle promptings in the right direction.

25 The grace of the Lord Jesus Christ be with your spirit.

be with your spirit

This means, "be with you."

This is Paul's characteristic final blessing. He concluded all 13 of his letters with a one-sentence blessing similar to the one here.

Glimpses into the Early Church from Philemon

Paul's letter to Philemon tells us many things about the earliest churches. These are glimpses into the life of the church; they are not fully-formed doctrines. In this letter, we learn that the church is to be a place of:

- Suffering for Christ (1, 23)
- Gatherings in homes (2)
- Accountability (2)
- Prayer (4)
- Deep familial relationships (5, 16)
- Love for one another (5)
- Life in Christ (5-6)
- Hospitality (7)
- Generosity (7, 14)
- Servanthood (8-9)
- Empowerment (8-9)
- How to make an appeal (8-12)
- Conflict resolution (9)
- Outreach to the lost (10)
- Building the next generation (10-11)
- Leader development (10-11)
- Trust in God's providence (15)
- Rejection of slavery (16)

- Equality between the brethren, in spite of social mores to the contrary (16)
- Love toward those who society has rejected (16)
- The church's response toward social change (16)
- The church's separation from the world (16)
- No sacred-secular distinction (16)
- Substitution, forgiveness and reconciliation (17-19)
- Healthy leadership authority (17-18)
- Leading in community (23-24)

All of these things are expressions of healthy church culture, and they are expressed in the letter in thoroughly practical ways. Notably, there is nothing in the letter about programs or organizational strategies, structures or forms; there is just life.

God and Slavery

SLAVERY IN NEW TESTAMENT TIMES

Slavery was a deeply entrenched practice in the world of the New Testament. The institution was universal in the Near East and in the Mediterranean world, and an estimated one-in-four people or more were slaves.[17] Nearly everyone in the Roman Empire took the institution of slavery for granted, except early Stoics who said that it was "against nature."

> This evil of slavery was so thoroughly interwoven with the entire domestic and public life of the heathen world, and so deliberately regarded, even by the greatest philosophers, Aristotle[18] for instance, as natural and indispensable, that the abolition of it, even if desirable, seemed to belong among the impossible things.[19]

17 In some agricultural regions, slaves comprised more than half the population! Because of this vast number of slaves, the Romans lived in constant fear of slave conspiracies and insurrections.

18 Aristotle wrote, "It is manifest therefore that there are cases of people of whom some are freemen and the others slaves by nature, and for these slavery is an institution both expedient and just." (Aristotle. (1944). *Aristotle in 23 Volumes, translated by H. Rackham.* (Vol. 21). Medford, MA: Cambridge, MA, Harvard University Press; London, William Heinemann Ltd.)

19 Schaff, P., & Schaff, D. S. (1910). *History of the Christian Church* (Vol. 2, p. 348). New York: Charles Scribner's Sons.

Unlike in the modern western world, slavery then was not based on an assumption of racial inferiority. Rather it was more of an economic matter – the slave might be the plunder from a military conquest, a criminal, someone who defaulted on debts, or simply one born into a slave family.

Roman law acknowledged that slaves were persons by nature, but from an economic standpoint they were treated as property. Their treatment was dependent on the master's goodness, or lack thereof, and many were treated severely. The master could legally execute his slaves, and they would all be executed if the master were murdered.

Even their family life was under the master's control. Slaves had no legal standing and their marriages were not legal contracts. Slaves were often abused sexually. Procreation was only to happen with the master's consent and then the children became his property. Sometimes the slaves would suffer having their family broken up and the children given away or sold.

In the Greco-Roman world, owning slaves was not limited to the rich; many households included at least one slave. The Greeks and Romans both employed a system in which slaves could own property, earn money, and buy their freedom, after saving enough money. Sometimes they were freed by the master in his will as a benefit for years of faithful service and as a token of generosity.

After freedom, slaves were still looked down upon and, while free to do many things, did not enjoy the full rights of Roman citizenship. The children of freed slaves, however, enjoyed the privileges of Roman citizenship without restrictions.

PROGRESSIVE REVELATION

While God allowed slavery in Israel in the Old Testament (e.g., Ex. 21:20-21; Lev. 25:44-46), that does not mean it was His highest will. In order to understand this, we must first understand *progressive revelation.*

For example, Jesus' words in the Sermon on the Mount are frequently misunderstood:

> *"You have heard that it was said, 'An eye for an eye and a tooth for a tooth.' But I say to you, 'Do not resist the one who is evil. But if anyone slaps you on the right cheek, turn to him the other also.'" (Matt. 5:38-39)*

Jesus quotes from the Law of Moses and says, "But I say to you ..." He appears to contradict the Law. When taken in the context of the entire Bible, however, we see that Jesus' statement does not represent a contradiction but rather a progression and deepening of ethical thought.

Before the Law, unlimited revenge ruled the earth. This is seen in several statements in Genesis 4:

> *Then the Lord said to him, "Not so! If anyone kills Cain, vengeance shall be taken on him sevenfold." And the Lord put a mark on Cain, lest any who found him should attack him. (Gen. 4:15)*
>
> *Lamech said to his wives: "Adah and Zillah, hear my voice; you wives of Lamech, listen to what I say: I have killed a man for wounding me, a young man for striking me. If Cain's revenge is sevenfold, then Lamech's is seventy-sevenfold." (Gen. 4:23-24)*

Then, when Moses gave the Law to Israel, that revenge was limited by justice. No longer was it acceptable to avenge one wrong with a greater retribution:

> *But if there is harm, then you shall pay life for life, eye for eye, tooth for tooth, hand for hand, foot for foot, burn for burn, wound for wound, stripe for stripe. (Ex. 21:23-25)*

Ultimately, when Jesus came, He took retribution for wrongs to its highest level – the level of grace and forgiveness:

> *"You have heard that it was said, 'An eye for an eye and a tooth for a tooth.' But I say to you, 'Do not resist the one who is evil. But if anyone slaps you on the right cheek, turn to him the other also.'" (Matt. 5:38-39)*

This is not a contradiction, but a *progressive* revelation. The ethical standard has progressed from unlimited retribution to limited retribution to forgiveness – from revenge to justice to mercy.

THE BIBLE AND SLAVERY

This idea of progressive revelation is also true regarding how God dealt with slavery. In biblical times, slavery was a normal part of society. But before the Law of Moses, slavery was unrestrained. Then, in the Law of Moses, God allowed slavery while limiting it and regulating it (e.g., Ex. 21:2-11; Lev. 25:39-46). Finally, in the New Testament, we see the equality of all men set forth (Gal. 3:28; Phm. 15-16).

In fact, both Testaments teach clearly against slavery:

> *Say therefore to the people of Israel, "I am the Lord, and I will bring you out from under the burdens of the Egyptians, and I will deliver you from slavery to them, and I will redeem you with an outstretched arm and with great acts of judgment." (Ex. 6:6)*
>
> *Whoever steals a man and sells him, and anyone found in possession of him, shall be put to death. (Ex. 21:16)*
>
> *If your brother becomes poor beside you and sells himself to you, you shall not make him serve as a slave: he shall be with you as a hired worker and as a sojourner. He shall serve with you until the year of the jubilee. Then he shall go out from you, he and his children with him, and go back to his own clan and return to the possession of his fathers. For they are My servants, whom I brought out of the land of Egypt; they shall not be sold as slaves. You shall not rule over him ruthlessly but shall fear your God. (Lev. 25:39-43)*
>
> *You shall not give up to his master a slave who has escaped from his master to you. He shall dwell with you, in your midst, in the place*

that he shall choose within one of your towns, wherever it suits him. You shall not wrong him. (Deut. 23:15-16)

If a man is found stealing one of his brothers of the people of Israel, and if he treats him as a slave or sells him, then that thief shall die. So you shall purge the evil from your midst. (Deut. 24:7)

Woe to him who builds his house by unrighteousness, and his upper rooms by injustice, who makes his neighbor serve him for nothing and does not give him his wages … (Jer. 22:13)

There is neither Jew nor Greek, there is neither slave nor free, there is no male and female, for you are all one in Christ Jesus. (Gal. 3:28)

… understanding this, that the law is not laid down for the just but for the lawless and disobedient, for the ungodly and sinners, for the unholy and profane, for those who strike their fathers and mothers, for murderers, the sexually immoral, men who practice homosexuality, enslavers ["slave traders"], liars, perjurers, and whatever else is contrary to sound doctrine … (1 Tim. 1:9-10)

For this perhaps is why he was parted from you for a while, that you might have him back forever, no longer as a slave but more than a slave, as a beloved brother – especially to me, but how much more to you, both in the flesh and in the Lord. (Phm. 15-16)

And the merchants of the earth weep and mourn for her, since no one buys their cargo anymore … cinnamon, spice, incense, myrrh, frankincense, wine, oil, fine flour, wheat, cattle and sheep, horses and chariots, and slaves, that is, human souls. (Rev. 18:11, 13)

The New Testament embraces the tension between the temporal social reality in the world of that day where slavery was a part of life (1 Cor. 7:20-24) and the eternal spiritual reality in the Church in which there are "neither slave nor free" (Gal. 3:28; Col. 3:11) and all are equal (Eph. 6:9).

On one hand, slaves and masters are given instructions in the New Testament on how to live their lives *as slaves and masters* now in the light of their commitment to Christ and of Jesus' very soon return (1 Cor. 7:31).

> *Each one should remain in the condition in which he was called. Were you a slave when called? Do not be concerned about it. (But if you can gain your freedom, avail yourself of the opportunity.) For he who was called in the Lord as a slave is a freedman of the Lord. Likewise he who was free when called is a slave of Christ. You were bought with a price; do not become slaves of men. So, brothers, in whatever condition each was called, there let him remain with God. (1 Cor. 7:20-24)*

> *Slaves, obey your earthly masters with fear and trembling, with a sincere heart, as you would Christ, not by the way of eye-service, as people-pleasers, but as slaves of Christ, doing the will of God from the heart, rendering service with a good will as to the Lord and not to man, knowing that whatever good anyone does, this he will receive back from the Lord, whether he is a slave or is free. Masters, do the same to them, and stop your threatening, knowing that He who is both their Master and yours is in heaven, and that there is no partiality with Him. (Eph. 6:5-9; see also Col. 3:22 – 4:1; 1 Tim. 6:1-2; Tit. 2:9; 1 Pet. 2:18-25)*

Paul did not tell the slaves to rebel and fight for their freedom, but to serve God faithfully in their current situation. Of course, if a slave can gain his freedom then he should do so!

> *Were you a slave when called? Do not be concerned about it. (But if you can gain your freedom, avail yourself of the opportunity.) (1 Cor. 7:21)*

On the other hand, in his letter to Philemon we see the expression of Paul's hope that there will be no slavery even now among the redeemed because in Christ we are all one. In fact, Paul's request of Philemon went beyond other documents of his time in not only pleading for clemency for a runaway slave but appealing that he be released.[20]

> *For this perhaps is why he was parted from you for a while, that you might have him back forever, no longer as a slave but more than a slave, as a beloved brother – especially to me, but how much more to you, both in the flesh and in the Lord. (Phm. 15-16)*

20 So clear and powerful was the message of the Bible that many of the earliest U.S. slaveholders did not want their slaves to be exposed to Christianity for fear that they would be compelled to free them. The Christian message had to be corrupted to make it neutral or supportive of slavery (Raboteau, Albert J., (1978), *Slave Religion.* New York: Oxford University Press). A "Slave Bible" was published in London in 1807 on behalf of the Society for the Conversion of Negro Slaves. They used the Slave Bible to teach the African slaves toiling in the Caribbean how to read while also introducing them to Christianity. However, the publishers of the Slave Bible removed portions of the Bible, such as the Exodus story, that could inspire hope for liberation. Instead, they emphasized passages that justified and strengthened the system of slavery that the British Empire needed.

SLAVERY AND THE EARLY CHURCH

Following Paul's teaching, the Early Church recognized no status difference between slave and master. All people were to be seated together. The word "slave," although very common among the graves of non-Christians, is never used in inscriptions in the Christian burials in the catacombs.

Christianity spread freely among slaves and they were often the instrument of salvation for their masters, especially among the women and children whose training was commonly entrusted to them. Many slaves died as martyrs for Christ. Slaves were also permitted to hold leadership roles in the Church; in fact, Callistus, a former slave, even became the bishop of the church of the city of Rome in AD 218-223!

According to Ignatius, a second-century bishop, church funds were used to buy freedom for slaves.[21] Some Christians even surrendered their freedom to ransom others from slavery.[22] Marriage among slaves was protected, and non-Christians were urged to free their slaves or allow them to purchase their own freedom. There are recorded examples of hundreds, and even thousands, of slaves being freed at a time, when a very wealthy master came to the Lord and, recognizing the equality of all men, set all his slaves free.

---

21 "And such sums of money as are collected from them in the manner aforesaid, appoint to be laid out in the redemption of the saints, the deliverance of slaves, and of captives, and of prisoners, and of those that have been abused, and of those that have been condemned by tyrants to single combat and death on account of the name of Christ. For the Scripture says: 'Deliver those that are led to death, and redeem those that are ready to be slain, do not spare.'" (*Constitutions of the Holy Apostles 4:9*)

22 "We know that many among ourselves have delivered themselves to bondage, that they might ransom others. Many have sold themselves to slavery, and receiving the price paid for themselves have fed others." (*1 Clement 55:2*)

… we read in the Acts of the martyrdom of the Roman bishop Alexander, that a Roman prefect, Hermas, converted by that bishop, in the reign of Trajan, received baptism at an Easter festival with his wife and children and twelve hundred and fifty slaves, and on this occasion gave all his slaves their freedom and munificent gifts besides. So in the martyrology of St. Sebastian, it is related that a wealthy Roman prefect, Chromatius, under Diocletian, on embracing Christianity, emancipated fourteen hundred slaves, after having them baptized with himself, because their sonship with God put an end to their servitude to man. Several epitaphs in the catacombs mention the fact of manumission [emancipation]. In the beginning of the fourth century St. Cantius, Cantianus, and Cantianilla, of an old Roman family, set all their slaves, seventy-three in number, at liberty, after they had received baptism. St. Melania emancipated eight thousand slaves; St. Ovidius, five thousand; Hermes, a prefect in the reign of Trajan, twelve hundred and fifty.[23]

Later, the freeing of slaves was so significant that it became a ritualistic act in churches.[24]

Thus, while the Early Church never sought to accomplish institutional change[25] – it was only after Constantine that the Church began to attack the institution of slavery itself – the equality of all men in

23 Schaff, P., & Schaff, D. S. (1910). *History of the Christian Church* (Vol. 2, pp. 352–353). New York: Charles Scribner's Sons.

24 "After the third century the manumission became a solemn act, which took place in the presence of the clergy and the congregation. It was celebrated on church festivals, especially on Easter. The master led the slave to the altar; there the document of emancipation was read, the minister pronounced the blessing, and the congregation received him as a free brother with equal rights and privileges. Constantine found this custom already established, and African councils of the fourth century requested the emperor to give it general force. He placed it under the superintendence of the clergy." (Schaff, P., & Schaff, D. S. (1910). *History of the Christian Church* (Vol. 2, pp. 353–354). New York: Charles Scribner's Sons.)

25 "Ancient Christianity was not especially concerned with forms of social liberation. … Emancipation simply never was and never became a goal of ancient Christianity." (Harper, Kyle. (2011). *Slavery in the Late Roman World* AD 275-425 (pp. 471-473). Cambridge, U.K.: Cambridge University Press.)

Christ was well established in the Church. According to Schaff, "Christianity almost obliterated the distinction between the two classes of society."[26]

At the same time, church leaders continued to exhort slaves the same way that Paul had – to serve God and find freedom in Christ in the midst of their current situation.

For example, Ignatius wrote to Polycarp:

> Do not despise either male or female slaves, yet neither let them be puffed up with conceit, but rather let them submit themselves the more, for the glory of God, that they may obtain from God a better liberty. Let them not long to be set free [from slavery] at the public expense, that they be not found slaves to their own desires.[27]

Tertullian wrote that outward freedom was worthless without the inward freedom of the soul from the bondage of sin.

> How can the world make a servant free? All is mere show in the world, nothing truth. For the slave is already free, as a purchase of Christ; and the freedman is a servant of Christ. If thou takest the freedom which the world can give for true, thou hast thereby become again the servant of man, and hast lost the freedom of Christ, in that thou thinkest it bondage.[28]

Thus, Paul's words in 1 Corinthians 7:20-24 are not in any way a condoning of slavery. Paul simply faces the reality of it. Moreover, his fundamental agenda was not a temporal, political one, but an eternal one. Therefore, if a slave can become free then he should

---

26 For an excellent study of the Church and slavery in the first three centuries after Christ, please see Schaff, P., & Schaff, D. S. (1910). *History of the Christian Church* (Vol. 2, pp. 348-353). New York: Charles Scribner's Sons.

27 Roberts, A., Donaldson, J., & Coxe, A. C. (Eds.). (1885). *The Apostolic Fathers with Justin Martyr and Irenaeus* (Vol. 1, pp. 94-95). Buffalo, NY: Christian Literature Company.

28 Schaff, P., & Schaff, D. S. (1910). *History of the Christian Church* (Vol. 2, p. 349). New York: Charles Scribner's Sons.

do so (1 Cor. 7:21) and, in the Church, believers should accept each other as brothers and not as slaves (Gal. 3:28; Col. 3:11; Phm. 15-16). However, those slaves who will not be set free should continue to serve God with all their heart and build up a greater inheritance in the true life that is soon to come.

THE CHRISTIAN AND SOCIAL CHANGE

The issue of slavery provides us with a very practical example of how the New Testament and then the Early Church approached social change in general.

Jesus spoke deeply of the personal responsibilities of His followers to walk righteously and justly, and in a way that glorifies God. Moreover, He said that His followers would be "salt" and "light" impacting the world around them.

> *You are the salt of the earth. But if the salt loses its saltiness, how can it be made salty again? It is no longer good for anything, except to be thrown out and trampled underfoot.*
>
> *You are the light of the world. A town built on a hill cannot be hidden. Neither do people light a lamp and put it under a bowl. Instead they put it on its stand, and it gives light to everyone in the house.*
>
> *In the same way, let your light shine before others, that they may see your good deeds and glorify your Father in heaven. (Matt. 5:13-16)*

Clearly, for us to be salt and light relates to our own lives and our personal impact on those around us.

Jesus never initiated a political movement that sought social change. In fact, at one critical moment, He specifically declined that opportunity:

> *Jesus answered, "My Kingdom is not of this world. If My Kingdom were of this world, My servants would have been fighting, that I*

might not be delivered over to the Jews. But My Kingdom is not from the world." (John 18:36; see also Matt. 26:52; John 6:15)

Jesus did, however, provide an extraordinary example of being salt and light as He gave His time, love, friendship and healing to the dispossessed. He gathered with the poor, prostitutes, tax collectors, women, lepers, Samaritans, Gentiles. He reached out to those who had been neglected and abused by society.

Thus, Jesus drew a clear distinction. The Christian is to walk with God, righteously and justly, in his own life and community. He is to be utterly different from the world and its ways. He is to serve those who have been abused by those in power. In doing so, he will have a profound impact on everyone around him. He will change his world.

We see the same clear vision in Paul. He called believers to walk deeply with God in truth and righteousness, to do good to all men (Gal. 6:10), and to change the lives of those around them by their lives and by their words as they shared the Gospel of hope and made disciples. Like Jesus, Paul reached out to the neglected and abused – the Gentiles, the poor, the disabled, prisoners, children, the elderly, slaves, women. But he also never sought institutional reform.

This explains why Paul accepted the fact that slavery was a part of the social order of his time and he instructed both slaves and masters how to live appropriately as believers within that social order (Eph. 6:5-9; Col. 3:22 – 4:1; 1 Tim. 6:1-2; 1 Pet. 2:18-25). Paul never tried to change the social institution of slavery. At the same time, he instructed Philemon to set Onesimus free – a profound request in that day!

The fact that Paul didn't try to change the social institution of slavery in no way meant that he condoned it. His moral rejection of slavery was reflected in his letter to Philemon and elsewhere in his writings. He taught that slave trading was a vile sin (1 Tim. 1:10). He affirmed the absolute equality before God of both master and slave (Eph. 6:9), and that there are "neither slave nor free" in Christ (Gal. 3:28; Col. 3:11). And he instructed Philemon to treat Onesimus "no longer as a slave but … as a beloved brother" (Phm. 16).

However, he knew his calling was not to try to reform the kingdoms of man but rather to call men into the Kingdom of God.

Then the Early Church, following both Jesus' and Paul's examples and teaching, did the same thing.

They often released slaves if they owned them. They purchased freedom for slaves. They worked hard to serve those who were oppressed. The Early Church believed – as Jesus and Paul did – in the equality of all men in Christ, and they lived in a way that aligned with this truth as salt and light in their communities. They were not passive. They were not just inward-looking. Slavery mattered greatly to them. They were salt and light. They did good to all men. They were very active and they sought to do justice, and to love kindness, and to walk humbly with their God (Mic. 6:8).

It was only after Constantine that the Church began to attack the institution of slavery itself.[29] By that time deep change had occurred in society broadly regarding slavery. The Church had profoundly impacted its world.

> But the church before Constantine labored with great success to elevate the intellectual and moral condition of the slaves, to adjust inwardly the inequality between slaves and masters, as the first and efficient step towards the final outward abolition of the evil, and to influence the public opinion even of the heathens. Here the church was aided by a concurrent movement in philosophy and legislation. The cruel views of Cato, who advised to work the slaves, like beasts of burden, to death rather than allow them to

29 For a broad study of slavery at the time, please see Harper, Kyle. (2011). *Slavery in the Late Roman World* ad 275-425. Cambridge, U.K.: Cambridge University Press.

> become old and unprofitable, gave way to the milder and humane views of Seneca, Pliny, and Plutarch, who very nearly approach the apostolic teaching. To the influence of the later Stoic philosophy must be attributed many improvements in the slave-code of imperial Rome. But the most important improvements were made from the triumph of Constantine to the reign of Justinian, under directly Christian influences.[30]

In conclusion, Paul's letter to Philemon shows us the true meaning of the Christian's calling to be "salt" and "light." It does not focus on alignment with political parties and human attempts at social reform. Jesus, Paul and the Early Church did not do that.[31] In their own lives and communities, however, they lived in a way that was radically different from the world around them, serving the dispossessed, challenging the social norms and calling people to come to Christ and, in Him, to live on a much higher moral plane, all while setting their eyes on the true eternal Kingdom.[32]

---

30 Schaff, P., & Schaff, D. S. (1910). *History of the Christian Church* (Vol. 2, pp. 349–350). New York: Charles Scribner's Sons.

31 "Paul was no William Wilberforce, but without Paul we might never have had William Wilberforce." (Bird, M. F. (2009). *Colossians and Philemon* (p. 30). Eugene, OR: Cascade Books.)

32 Just as Paul told the slaves of his time, "If you can gain your freedom, avail yourself of the opportunity" (1 Cor. 7:21), likewise, if God calls you to a position of institutional power (e.g., congressman, mayor, police chief) then you should certainly use that opportunity to bring institutional reform as you are able. However, for most Christians, the primary expression of being "salt" and "light" should be in the hard work of their own lives and relationships, as they take personal responsibility to bring change around them through loving and serving the dispossessed and marginalized.

www.ingramcontent.com/pod-product-compliance
Lightning Source LLC
LaVergne TN
LVHW010108110826
845155LV00028B/537